SHOES !

Printed in the United States

9 8 7 6 5 4 3 2 1

Digit on the right indicates the number of this printing.

ISBN 0-7624-0696-8

Cover and interior illustrations by Beth Adams
Designed by Bryn Ashburn
Edited by Caroline Tiger

This book may be ordered by mail from the publisher.
Please include $2.50 for postage and handling.
But try your bookstore first!

Running Press Book Publishers
125 South Twenty-second Street
Philadelphia, Pennsylvania 19103-4399

Visit us on the web!
www.runningpress.com

SHOES!

A Personal Journal, with Heart and Sole

RUNNING PRESS
PHILADELPHIA · LONDON

In one lifetime, each of us
may walk 65,000 miles—
nearly two-and-one-half times
around the world.

Laurie Lawlor
American writer

The foot itself is the starting point
of a wonderful series of inventions.

Otis Tufton Mason (1838–1908)
American ethnologist

*Nothing has been invented yet that will do
a better job than heels at making a good pair of legs
look great, or great ones look fabulous.*

Stuart Weitzman
American fashion designer

[A] person having on India rubber shoes
need have little apprehension
of danger from lightning.

Charles Goodyear (1800–1860)
American inventor

Shoes, and not men, are God's gift to women.

Mimi Pond
American cartoonist

*Every woman may be shod like a princess
and every princess may be shod like a fairy queen.*

Salvatore Ferragamo (1898–1960)
Italian shoe designer

Her fairy godmother had scarcely touched Cinderella
with her wand when her rags changed into a gown of gold and silver,
embroidered with rubies, pearls, and diamonds.
Then she gave her a pair of little glass slippers—the prettiest in the whole world.

Cinderella
Charles Perrault (1628–1703)
French Writer

To be carried by shoes, winged by them.
To wear dreams on one's feet is to begin
to give reality to one's dreams.

Roger Vivier
French shoe designer

Even the least vain among us has been known to blow
an entire week's salary on an irresistible new pair.

Linda O'Keeffe
American journalist

The more shoes I get, the more I want.

Amy Fine Collins
American writer

The little Princess stood on a balcony so that (everyone) could see her,
dressed in white. She had no train or golden crown,
but she was wearing beautiful red shoes made of morocco leather. . . .
There was nothing like those red shoes in all the world!

The Red Shoes
Hans Christian Anderson (1805–1875)
Danish writer

Once upon a time there was a king who had twelve daughters,
one more beautiful than the next. They slept together in a large room,
where their beds stood side by side, and in the evening, when they went to sleep,
the king shut and locked the door. However, when he opened it in the morning,
he would see that their shoes were worn out from dancing,
and nobody could discover how this kept happening.

The Worn Out Dancing Shoes
Jacob Grimm (1785–1863) and Wilhelm Grimm (1786–1859)
German writers

Pointe shoes seem to have a life of their own,
incidentally, and each different ballet has
an effect on the life of the shoe.

Melissa Hayden
Canadian ballerina

Ballet shoes have no right or left feet. When they are new,
they are interchangeable until the dancer works them in and decides which
goes better on which foot. They should more accurately be called slippers,
as they are derived from the light silk slippers worn by fashionable
ladies to evening dances in the last century.

Margot Fonteyn (1919–1991)
English ballerina

Who can ever have enough shoes?
Maybe you can squeeze a couple
more pairs under the bed!

Brooke Shields
American actor

Short women aren't given any respect. People think we're cute.
But when you put on a pair of 4-inch platforms, people give you a different reaction–
especially men. I become a different person when I put on my platforms.

Tracy Chalfa
American entrepeneur

Marie Antoinette, the French queen who met her fate on the guillotine in 1793, kept a servant whose only job was looking after the sovereign's 500 pairs of shoes.

In the early 17th century, traveling noblemen wore shoes with hollow heels, in which they hid valuables from highwaymen and thieves.

I wear a different pair of shoes every night. It's funny because
when I explain why I do that, everyone can relate. . . . You feel energized,
you feel a little better about yourself. That's why I started doing it. I didn't do that
my first year. But as I started putting on a new pair of shoes I felt like,
"I'm walking out there with my own shoes and I'm happy as hell."

Michael Jordan
American athlete

Estimated from a wife's experience,
the average man spends fully one-quarter
of his life in looking for his shoes.

Helen Rowland (1875–1950)
American journalist

If they are stylish, we feel stylish, and to hell with comfort.

Colin McDowell
English fashion historian

Shoes were often creations of fantasy.
Designers made "invisible" shoes with transparent plastics,
and high cantilevered shoes that were supported
only at the toe and had no heel.

David Yue
American historian

lace into

on a shoe string

shoestring budget

walking tall

footloose and
fancy free

follow in her footsteps

stepping out

head over heels

cold feet

fancy footwork

(Fashionable American women) . . .
walk in the middle of the winter with their
poor little toes pinched into a miniature slipper,
incapable of excluding as much moisture as
might bedew a primrose.

Frances Milton Trollope (1780–1863)
English writer

*Shoes are the exclamation point
at the end of a fashion statement.*

Laurie Schecter
American writer

The wealthiest woman in the world couldn't
pay me to make her an ugly pair of shoes.

André Perugia (1893–1977)
French shoe designer

Alienation and rebellion were shown by wearing
outrageous shoes—steel-capped or zippered shoes—
or just by writing slogans on a pair of shoes.

Charlotte Yue
American historian

I'd like to expand my costume-wearing as I age.
Let's all wear bright togas, wild shoes, flabbergasting hats
and meet in a drumming circle, in a forest near
a hot spring. All costumes welcome!

Sark
American writer

You cannot put the same shoe on every foot.

Publius Syrus
1st century B.C. Greek philosopher

Shoes transform one so much more
easily and conveniently than weekend
seminars, bestseller hardbacks,
aerobics, bee pollen, or the Right Man.

Mimi Pond
American cartoonist

It would be a big mistake to assume that people are forming opinions
of you in terms of your hair, clothes, or makeup, or making assumptions based on
your no-doubt incomprehensible-to-earthlings description of your work,
or in terms of where you live, or with whom you are mated.
The truly attuned jump to conclusions based on shoes.

Anne Beattie
American writer

Mama always said there's an awful lot you can tell about a person by their shoes: where they're going, where they've been.

Without shoes, our ambitions would fade away, wolfish trade practices seem too much trouble, international frictions look foolish. Armies would curl up to take a nap. Nobody would get any serious work done and the world would go straight to hell.

Barbara Holland
American writer

Shoes reveal many things about
the physical appearance, the personality,
and the character of the wearer.
Shoes can be artistic; they can be witty.
Like all good design, shoes can
enhance the quality of life.

Charlotte Yue
American historian

If you look inside any well-worn shoe, you see indentations left
by the owner's toes and concave hollows worn smooth by the heel.
The scarred sole of the shoe is evidence of the posture, gait,
and number of miles traveled by its owner.

Nancy Rexford
American historian

Please send me your last pair of shoes,
already worn out in dancing . . . so that I might
have something to press against my heart.

Johann Wolfgang von Goethe (1749–1832)
German poet

Ancient Greeks didn't mail valentines to express
their devotion. They carved their beloved's name
on the soles of their sandals. Wherever they walked,
the names were imprinted in the dust.

Laurie Lawlor
American writer

What color was her hair? What did her eyes look like?
I have no idea. But the burgundy gillies that shoed her foot
underneath are blazed on my memory.

Chip Brown
American journalist

I'll take a look at your slippers.
I love them as much as I do you . . .
I smell their perfume,
they smell of verbena.

Gustave Flaubert (1821–1880)
French writer

*Women may scour the world
for the shoes of their hearts' desire,
but it's men who swoon at their feet.*

Jody Shields
American writer

Roger Vivier's shoes transformed the most humble of human appendages
into ethereal, aerodynamic fantasies, as gossamer as dragonflys' wings
and as carefully calibrated as a suspension bridge.
He had one foot in the Middle Ages, the other beyond the future.

Amy Fine Collins
American writer

Ancient Egyptians believed that inhaling smoke
from a burning sandal would cure a headache.

In colonial America, a remedy for a stomachache
was lying down with a heavy pair of boots on the abdomen.

Now Maria pushed the door all the way open, but instead of ushering him inside, she leaned up against the doorjamb and crossed her legs and folded her arms underneath her breasts and kept staring at him and chuckling. She was wearing high-heeled pumps with a black-and-white checkerboard pattern worked into the leather. Sherman knew little about shoe designs, but it registered on him that this one was of the moment.

Bonfire of the Vanities
Tom Wolfe
American writer

Shoes are candy for the eyes, poetry for feet, icing
on your soul. They stand for everything you've ever wanted:
glamour, success, a rapierlike wit, a date with
the SexGod of your choice, Barbie's wedding dress.

Mimi Pond
American cartoonist

What a good shoe crucially does, must do, is reveal the foot,
enhance and display it, offer a frame and a setting for it. And that
is precisely the nature of my erotic obsession. I crave the intersection
of art and nature, of the human body and the created object,
the foot and the shoe, flesh and leather . . .

Geoff Nicholson
American writer

A New Orleans madam first imported
the French high heel to America in the 1880s
when she saw how it improved her business.

Christa Worthington
American writer

It's hard not to be sexy in a pair of high heels.

Tom Ford
American designer for Gucci

People walk differently in high heels . . .
You walk in a sensuous way.
Your body sways to a different kind of tempo.

Manolo Blahnik
Spanish-born English shoe designer

High heels put
your ass on a pedestal
—where it belongs.

Veronica Webb
American fashion model

How tall am I? Honey, with hair, heels, and attitude, I'm through the damned roof.

RuPaul
American entertainer

Who has ever seen a street hooker, a drag queen,
or a male transvestite in flats?

Charles Panati
American writer

When I walk out the door in a good pair of high heels . . .
I never feel vulnerable, there's no time for any weakness, I feel focused,
strong, secure, my stride is potent and no one hassles me when I'm standing
on the corner hailing a cab . . . I demand respect and my heels back me up
—so don't go worrying about me, I've never been better, care for a cigar?

Sandra Bernhard
American entertainer

Ever since I was very young, I have been obsessed with spike heels. The allegorical interpretation that Almodovar gives in his film *High Heels* —of the sound of footsteps that the heroine associates with the memory of her mother—seems to me to convey marvelously the infinite resonances of the sensory range.

Christian Louboutin
French shoe designer

I adore girls in high heels. They can wear high heels and we can't.
It's the one thing that differentiates men and women.

Mario Testino
American fashion photographer

Sensible shoes command respect, but high heels solicit adoration.
A Birkenstock may offer deliverance, but a Blahnik promises adventure.

Linda O'Keeffe
American writer

I don't know who invented the high heel,
but all women owe him a lot.

Marilyn Monroe (1926–1962)
American actress

Not diamonds but heels are a girl's best friend.

William Rossi
American writer

If you rebel against high heels,
take care to do so in a very smart hat.

George Bernard Shaw (1856–1950)
Irish playwright

skip to my loo

dancing on air

feet first

tightlaced

twinkle toes

light on your feet

walking on sunshine

if the shoe fits

foot in mouth

best foot forward

The only coherent fashion statement I can recall from the entire
[women's] movement was the suggestion that Mrs. Cleaver,
Beaver's mom, would on the whole have been a happier woman
had she not persisted in vacuuming while wearing high heels.

Molly Ivins
American columnist

An athletic shoe signals that
you are a competitive person.

Anne Hollander
American historian

If you live in England, you say "trainers," and if you live in Australia, you say "sand shoes." There are many names for this comfortable, lightweight footwear, but the general name—the one that has been used since 1873—is sneakers.

Robert Young
American teacher

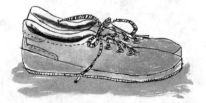

All of a sudden, French women who have never been shod in anything more décontracté than Inès de la Fressange moccasins are turning up in canvas Guess shoes, suede Pumas, old-school Adidas, even Skechers.

Guy Trebay
American journalist

Among the neon stripes and air pumps of contemporary sneakerdom, those who choose to wear humble, unadorned white Converse sneakers are the monks of sneakerland.

Stephen Talty
Sneaker aficionado

Variety in footwear is the wave of the future. As an advertisement
for Nine West put it in 1996: "We all need strappy, sexy, patent sandals.
Slinky, stretchy, comfy slings. Hip, lively loafers. Open toes, with plenty
of sole. Sassy, shine Mary Janes. We all need shoes."

Valerie Steele
American curator

Remember, it's ultimately more chic to wear
the same pair of glorious top-quality shoes every
day than a different pair of mediocre ones
every other. On the other hand, if you find
irresistible ones on sale . . .

Leah Feldon
American fashion consultant

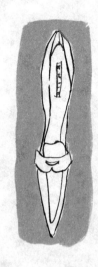

Shoes, like buildings,
have a mysterious chemistry
of proportion.

Suzanne Slesin
American writer

I'm mad for beautiful shoes and they must be well-maintained, kept on a mold and polished. Classic shoes in black and brown can look beautiful, but at times I like different colors—like the olive green used in old luggage and the interiors of old cars. Bright colors are good for sweaters, ties, and waistcoats.

Karl Lagerfeld
German fashion designer

In those days women wore high button shoes and to achieve a good fit, the buttons usually had to be adjusted for each customer. The clerk would mark the new positions for the buttons with a pencil.

Elmer Nordstrom
American businessman

Shoes are as important as the dress.
The balance of the heel gives the attitude
of the look. It is the pitch, the whole
rhythm that depends upon the shoe.

Norma Kamali
American fashion designer

The journey of a thousand miles
begins by finding your shoes.

Laotzu
1st century B.C. Chinese philosopher

When women ask me about heels,
I say, try a pair on. If you don't see
the magic, stick to Reeboks.

Manolo Blahnik
Spanish-born English shoe designer

You don't need ornamentation, only a certain delicacy
and refinement of details and materials.
Even women who love heels also like to wear flats sometimes,
and if done beautifully, flats can be very sophisticated and elegant.

Franco Fieramosca
Italian fashion designer

The wonderful thing about
flat sandals is that you have
the feeling of being barefoot.
It's pure liberation.

Christian Louboutin
French fashion designer

*If you look under the table
at any dinner party, most women
will have kicked their shoes off.*

Diego Della Valle
Spanish businessman

If I'm not in platforms, I'm barefoot. I feel like a giant in them. . . .
I will always wear platforms even when I'm ninety years old.

Traci Bingham
American actor

Shoes (in Renaissance-era Venice) became so high that when a lady went out she needed a maidservant to help keep her upright. Indeed the shoes's height was so formidable that laws were passed against such excesses.

Eugenia Girotti
Italian writer

If it's conservative, it's dead.

Vivienne Westwood
English fashion designer

Give a girl the correct footwear
and she can conquer the world.

Bette Midler
American entertainer

Our ability to accessorize
is what separates us from
the animals.

"Clairee Belcher"
from the film *Steel Magnolias*

It's easy to overload shoes, but the
essence should be about one good idea.
A beautiful buckle on a nice clean
shoe is probably the best example.

Patrick Cox
Canadian shoe designer

Women like to be protected,
and boots are a kind of armor.
I think this is why we sell
millions of boots.

Manolo Blahnik
Spanish-born English shoe designer

Put on thy boots, we'll ride all night.

No matter if they are stiletto or flat-heeled, black, or pink, knee-high
or demi-ankle, boots instill you with a certain Power.

Mimi Pond
American cartoonist

Knee-high boots are vampy. . . .
Guys see them and think,
"Ooh!" You're not going to get
that from wearing loafers.

Sharon Segal
Co-owner, Fred Segal store

A man's shoe made for a woman—that has since become the accessory equivalent of the little black dress, indispensable to a wardrobe.

Robert Clergerie
French shoe designer

The pump is the little black dress of the shoe world.

Linda O'Keeffe
American writer

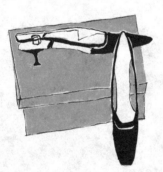

Perfect Black Pumps indicate a perfectly manicured soul.
They tell the world that you are in control of every phase of your life,
from your complexion to your financial assets
to any adolescents who might claim a close blood relationship to you
after they've been arrested for grand larceny.

Mimi Pond
American cartoonist

Dorothy now took Toto up solemnly in her arms, and having said one last good-bye she clapped the heels of her shoes together three times. "Take me home to Aunt Em!" Instantly she was whirling through the air, so swiftly that all she could see or feel was the wind whistling past her ears.

Lyman Frank Baum (1856–1919)
American writer

And one last warning:
Shoes can be addictive.
Ask Imelda.

Leah Feldon
American fashion consultant